DEFENDING OUR NATION

DEFENDING THE GROUND:
THE ARMY

Series Titles

CITIZEN SOLDIERS: THE NATIONAL GUARD

CUSTOMS AND BORDER PROTECTION

DEFENDING THE SKIES: THE AIR FORCE

DEFENDING THE GROUND: THE ARMY

DEFENDING THE SEAS: THE NAVY

THE DRUG ENFORCEMENT ADMINISTRATION

HOMELAND SECURITY

THE NATIONAL COUNTERTERRORISM CENTER

PROTECTING AGAINST BIOLOGICAL AND CHEMICAL ATTACK

PUTTING OUT FIRES: FIREFIGHTERS

RESCUING HOSTAGES: THE FBI

STOPPING CRIME: THE POLICE

DEFENDING OUR NATION

DEFENDING THE GROUND:
THE ARMY

FOREWORD BY
MANNY GOMEZ, ESQ., SECURITY AND TERRORISM EXPERT

BY
CHRIS MCNAB

MASON CREST

Mason Crest
450 Parkway Drive, Suite D
Broomall, PA 19008
www.masoncrest.com

Printed in the United States of America
First printing
9 8 7 6 5 4 3 2 1

Series ISBN: 978-1-4222-3759-5
Hardcover ISBN: 978-1-4222-3762-5
ebook ISBN: 978-1-4222-8018-8

Library of Congress Cataloging-in-Publication Data

Names: McNab, Chris, author.
Title: Defending the ground : the Army / FOREWORD BY MANNY GOMEZ, ESQ.,
  SECURITY AND TERRORISM EXPERT ; by Chris McNab.
Description: Broomall, Pennsylvania : MASON CREST, [2018] | Series: Defending our nation | Includes index.
Identifiers: LCCN 2016053126| ISBN 9781422237625 (hardback) | ISBN
  9781422237595 (series) | ISBN 9781422280188 (ebook)
Subjects: LCSH: United States. Army--Juvenile literature.
Classification: LCC UA25 .M23 2018 | DDC 355.00973--dc23

Additional Text: Kelly Kagamas Tomkies

CONTENTS

FOREWORD BY MANNY GOMEZ, ESQ. 6

1 HISTORY OF THE U.S. ARMY 8

2 MISSIONS AND COMMANDS OF THE
   U.S. ARMY 18

3 TRAINING FOR DEFENSE 30

4 WEAPONS OF THE U.S. ARMY 40

5 CHEMICAL, NUCLEAR, AND BIOLOGICAL
   DEFENSE 50

6 FIGHTING FOR FREEDOM ABROAD 56

7 THE WAR AGAINST TERRORISM 64

SERIES GLOSSARY 72

CHRONOLOGY 76

FURTHER RESOURCES 78

INDEX 79

ABOUT THE AUTHOR AND PICTURE CREDITS 80

KEY ICONS TO LOOK FOR:

Words to understand: These words with their easy-to-understand definitions will increase the reader's understanding of the text while building vocabulary skills.

Sidebars: This boxed material within the main text allows readers to build knowledge, gain insights, explore possibilities, and broaden their perspectives by weaving together additional information to provide realistic and holistic perspectives.

Educational Videos: Readers can view videos by scanning our QR codes, providing them with additional educational content to supplement the text. Examples include news coverage, moments in history, speeches, iconic sports moments and much more!

Text-dependent questions: These questions send the reader back to the text for more careful attention to the evidence presented there.

Research projects: Readers are pointed toward areas of further inquiry connected to each chapter. Suggestions are provided for projects that encourage deeper research and analysis.

Series glossary of key terms: This back-of-the book glossary contains terminology used throughout this series. Words found here increase the reader's ability to read and comprehend higher-level books and articles in this field.

FOREWORD

VIGILANCE

We live in a world where we have to have a constant state of awareness—about our surroundings and who is around us. Law enforcement and the intelligence community cannot predict or stop the next terrorist attack alone. They need the citizenry of America, of the world, to act as a force multiplier in order to help deter, detect, and ultimately defeat a terrorist attack.

Technology is ever evolving and is a great weapon in the fight against terrorism. We have facial recognition, we have technology that is able to detect electronic communications through algorithms that may be related to terrorist activity—we also have drones that could spy on communities and bomb them without them ever knowing that a drone was there and with no cost of life to us.

But ultimately it's human intelligence and inside information that will help defeat a potential attack. It's people being aware of what's going on around them: if a family member, neighbor, coworker has suddenly changed in a manner where he or she is suddenly spouting violent anti-Western rhetoric or radical Islamic fundamentalism, those who notice it have a duty to report it to authorities so that they can do a proper investigation.

In turn, the trend since 9/11 has been for international communication as well as federal and local communication. Gone are the days when law enforcement or intelligence organizations kept information to themselves and didn't dare share it for fear that it might compromise the integrity of the information or for fear that the other organization would get equal credit. So the NYPD wouldn't tell anything to the FBI, the FBI wouldn't tell the CIA, and the CIA wouldn't tell the British counterintelligence agency, MI6, as an example. Improved as things are, we could do better.

We also have to improve global propaganda. Instead of dropping bombs, drop education on individuals who are even considering joining ISIS. Education is salvation. We have the greatest production means in the world through Hollywood and so on, so why don't we match ISIS materials? We tried it once but the government itself tried to produce it. This is something that should definitely be privatized. We also need to match the energy of cyber attackers—and we need savvy youth for that.

There are numerous ways that you could help in the fight against terror—joining law enforcement, the military, or not-for-profit organizations like the Peace Corps. If making the world a safer place appeals to you, draw on your particular strengths and put them to use where they are needed. But everybody should serve and be part of this global fight against terrorism in some small way. Certainly, everybody should be a part of the fight by simply being aware of their surroundings and knowing when something is not right and acting on that sense. In the investigation after most successful attacks, we know that somebody or some persons or people knew that there was something wrong with the person or persons who perpetrated the attack. Although it feels awkward to tell the authorities that you believe somebody is acting suspicious and may be a terrorist sympathizer or even a terrorist, we have a higher duty not only to society as a whole but to our family, friends, and ultimately ourselves to do something to ultimately stop the next attack.

It's not *if* there is going to be another attack, but where, when, and how. So being vigilant and being proactive are the orders of the day.

Manny Gomez, Esq.
President of MG Security Services,
Chairman of the National Law Enforcement Association,
former FBI Special Agent, U.S. Marine, and NYPD Sergeant

CHAPTER 1

HISTORY OF THE U.S. ARMY

The infantry of the Continental Army.

The U.S. Army has been protecting the citizens of the United States at home and abroad for more than 240 years. From a tiny force of less than 1,000 men, it has grown into the largest and most powerful army in the world today.

The U.S. Army was created under the presidency of George Washington (1732–1799) on June 14, 1775, at the Second Continental Congress. The Revolutionary War (1775–1780) was just beginning, and the United States required a more organized military force to cast off British rule. As a result, the Continental Army was formed, commanded by a five-member **civilian** board. The army was small in size, initially numbering only 960 men, but, alongside various state militias, it ultimately defeated the British at Yorktown in 1780. Its job done, the army was officially disbanded on November 2, 1783.

President Washington now faced a problem. The young United States still required a national army to protect it, but one that would not threaten the military independence of the various states. In the 1780s, the United States relied on state militias for protection. These militias had fought hard during the Revolutionary War, but they did have their limitations. Militia soldiers were mostly laborers, which meant they could be called up for about 30–60 days only—any longer, and U.S. industry and agriculture suffered from a lack of manpower. Furthermore, the discipline and effectiveness of the militias varied tremendously.

Words to Understand

Civilian: Person not a member of the military, police, or other armed force.

Fortification: Structure built with the goal of protecting a specific area.

Truce: Agreement between opposing sides to end fighting.

These militias remained vital for the defense of the states, but the territory of the new United States was so vast that no single army could guard it. Washington realized that if the United States was to protect itself against the threat of invasion and internal conflict, and if it was to expand its western frontier, it needed a national army separate from state politics. So the U.S. Army was established, with Washington as its commander in chief. The state militias retained responsibility for their own localities, while the army was used to man coastal **fortifications** and open up new U.S. territories.

The Army Goes to War

The U.S. Army faced its first real military test in the War of 1812 (1812–1814) in which the United States fought against the British over territory and shipping rights. Though the army struggled at first against the highly organized British units, it eventually proved to be a competent fighting force. Its numbers expanded from about 6,000 men at the start of the war to 33,000 by 1815. State militias (numbering some 500,000 men) did play a vital role in the war, but the army often took the lion's share of the fighting. Its resilience led to a **truce** between Britain and the United States in 1814, and Britain finally gave up its attempt to influence U.S. affairs.

Following the war, the army worked hard to improve the quality of its leaders. More officers were sent to the United States' first military academy, West Point, in New York, which had been established in 1812. Their skills were soon tested in another conflict, the Mexican War (1846–1848). In almost every major battle against the Mexicans, the Army was victorious. Its actions were supported by more than 60,000 one-year volunteers from the various states, but its own size expanded to around 42,000 men. Despite the larger state force, the Army fought most of the major encounters and suffered more than 70 percent of the total U.S. casualties.

In 1861, the federal army faced its most unpleasant conflict, the American Civil War (1861–1865). The Civil War was a war of the masses, and the scale of the conflict was so

Soldiers of the Colored Infantry in 1865.

great that the regular army had a limited impact on its outcome. More than four million men fought, but less than 100,000 were U.S. Army regulars. When the war ended, the Army actually shrank in size, and by 1890 it was reduced to a force of only about 27,000 men. It could be expanded in times of crisis by the reserve army, called the National Guard, but this was independent from the federal government. The drop in numbers and low morale in the Army led to high U.S. casualties during the Spanish-American War (1898) and the Philippines insurrection (1899–1902).

Union Soldiers entrenched in the Battle of Chancellorsville.

The 20th Century

The first half of the 20th century saw steady changes in the U.S. Army. During the first two decades, its soldiers benefited from major leaps in military technology, including magazine rifles, machine guns, radio communications, new artillery, and the advent of military aviation. Officer-training schools grew in number, producing more men competent for leadership. Total soldier numbers grew to around 100,000 men by 1905 alone. Even so, the Army did not approach the scale of the major European armies, which were to face each other in World War I (1914–1918).

The United States did not enter the war until 1917, but even as battle lines were being drawn across Europe, the U.S. government realized the importance of a large army. The National Defense Act of 1916 authorized the Army to expand to 175,000 men in 111 regiments.

I WANT YOU
FOR U.S. ARMY
NEAREST RECRUITING STATION

Recruiting posters like this were common during World War I.

The National Guard, a special reserve element of the Army, grew to 400,000 members. During the war itself, the Army reached a total of 3,685,000 men, 75 percent of which were acquired through conscription under the Selective Service Act of 1917.

The U.S. Army fought with distinction during World War I. The war also saw the creation of the Air Service, an aviation wing of the Army. It was the next world war that would make the U.S. Army the most powerful force on Earth.

The United States entered World War II (1939–1945) in 1941, but it began preparations for war at the outset of hostilities in Europe. In 1939, much of the army's equipment was obsolete, and an economic depression meant that there were only 380,000 soldiers available. In 1940, the government made emergency plans to increase the size of the Army to 8.8 million in the case of war. When the United States went to war, the Army actually reached 11 million personnel, 4 million being ground forces; the rest were split between the United States Army Air Force and the Army Service Forces. U.S. industry also rose to the challenge of war and began producing equipment in awesome numbers and of superior quality. Without the Army's contribution, it is doubtful that Nazi Germany or Imperial Japan would have been defeated.

Action on Omaha Beach

On June 6, 1944, Allied forces stormed the beaches of Normandy, France, as part of a massive invasion of German-occupied Europe. There were five main landing areas, code-named Gold, Juno, Sword, Utah, and Omaha. It was at Omaha that the U.S. Army suffered a terrible slaughter. Omaha beach was six miles long and backed by cliffs 100 feet (33 m) high. The water and beach were heavily mined, and the German defenders were combat-hardened veterans. At 6:30 a.m. U.S. Army soldiers of the 1st Infantry Division and the 29th Division stormed ashore in assault boats into a hail of machine gun bullets and artillery fire; many were killed before they even stepped off the boats. Bodies soon littered the beach. Those who survived tried to find any cover they could. Finally, under the support of naval bombardment, the U.S. soldiers inched their way up the beach and stormed the cliffs. The German positions began to fall, and by nightfall, the U.S. Army had taken the beach. However, they suffered over 2,400 casualties, nearly half of the total Allied casualties suffered on D-Day.

The morning's battle in 1944 at Omaha Beach left many casualties in its wake.

A World War II veteran remembers D-Day.

World War II turned the U.S. Army into a modern, professional, and powerful military force. The end of the war resulted in a plunge in numbers to just 554,000 troops, but as the Cold War developed, the Army once more needed to grow. The threat now was the Soviet Union, and the war between U.S. democracy and Soviet Communism was fought in many different locations around the world. Within 20 years of the end of World War II, the U.S. Army had fought or entered into two major conflicts, the Korean War (1950–1952) and the Vietnam War (1964–1974). The constant commitments of the Army led to a peacetime strength of about one million personnel. Advances in the U.S. computer industry in the 1960s also enabled the Army to lead the world in military technology.

An Army Veteran Reflects on Battle

Ray Wells, a U.S. Army veteran of World War II and the Korean War, reflects poignantly on the personal effects of battle:

"I can only imagine what thoughts go through the young replacement when he reports to his company and sees what battle has done to the battle-hardened veteran. Many of these young men and boys, or most of them, rather, teenagers, never found their companies or knew a soul in their units, because in the heat of battle, in the dark, lonely and afraid, the enemy's bullet found them and they were no more. Perfect strangers to us. We sorrowed for these unknown comrades, but only their families, friends, wives, or sweethearts at home knew them. [We know] what battle and war really is, the sad, lonesome feeling of going back to the lines during the night, rain beating down on your face, fear in your hearts, and doing your best to not let the feeling [be] known to your buddies, and knowing that your comrades must be feeling the same way and would not let you down.

"I don't think I can really come up with the words so that the uninitiated can understand or even be interested, but I know the ones who went through these horrible experiences will understand what I am trying to say. Why were we, the living, allowed to come back; how were we chosen to continue with our lives when so many others made the extreme sacrifice and lie in those cemeteries, row upon row of crosses, so far away? God bless them and God bless all of you who are still suffering in your own way."

The defeat in Vietnam taught the Army some painful lessons because it bore a heavy share of the 58,000 U.S. personnel lost in the war. Since then, much of its effort has been channeled into peacekeeping and humanitarian and protective missions, though the Gulf War (1990–1991) and the war on terrorism in Afghanistan (2001–2014) have maintained the Army's combat expertise. Its soldiers, particularly those belonging to the special forces units, are regularly deployed overseas, protecting U.S. interests or democratic allies. Today's Army is backed by a current budget of more than $110 billion, making it the most financially stable and militarily advanced fighting force in the world. Though it has come a long way since 1775, the U.S. Army still has the same role: to ensure the peace and prosperity of the American people.

Text-Dependent Questions

1. Under whose presidency did the U.S. Army form?
2. Which act authorized the Army to increase its size during World War I?
3. Which country did the United States oppose during the Cold War?

Research Projects

1. The Vietnam War was highly unpopular among U.S. citizens. Research why the war was so unpopular and how U.S. citizens voiced their protests of the country's involvement.
2. Research the U.S. Army's role during the War on Terror in Afghanistan. How would you describe its role? Did it achieve its mission?

CHAPTER 2

MISSIONS AND COMMANDS OF THE U.S. ARMY

A U.S. Army soldier attends a training exercise.

The U.S. Army is a massive organization that needs strict lines of command if it is to function properly and efficiently. Ultimately, the leadership of the Army extends right back to the president of the United States.

The structure of the U.S. Army was established by the National Security Act of 1947 and its amendments in 1949. The 1947 Act altered the shape and composition of the Army. Most significantly, it transferred most of the Army's pilots and aircraft into the newly formed United States Air Force. The 1949 amendments set the relationship between the Army and the federal government.

At the top of the chain of command resides the National Command Authority, consisting of the president and the secretary of defense. The National Command Authority takes the final responsibility for U.S. military actions at home and abroad. The president is the commander in chief of the armed forces and has the final say on the operational deployments of all U.S. forces—Army, Navy, Marine Corps, and Air Force. The secretary of defense exercises control over the Department of Defense.

The U.S. Army Oath of Enlistment

The mission of the U.S. Army is best summarized in the oath of enlistment taken by all U.S. military personnel:

> I do solemnly swear that I will support and defend the Constitution of the United States against all enemies, foreign and domestic; that I will bear true faith and allegiance to the same; and that I will obey the orders of the President of the United States and the orders of the Officers appointed over me, according to regulations and the Uniform Code of Military Justice. So help me God!

This oath commits the soldier to defend U.S. citizens and interests at home and abroad.

Words to Understand

Allocation: Divide and distribute.

Integration: To make something part of something else.

Matériel: Military equipment, supplies.

At the U.S. Military Academy, new cadets take the Oath of Enlistment.

The Department of Defense has a vast range of roles, including the following:

- Developing policies that support the United States' security needs.
- Reviewing the condition of the armed forces and making changes to improve their readiness and capabilities.
- Overseeing the allocation of military budgets to the arms of service.
- Evaluating U.S. military actions and reviewing their accordance with national military and political objectives.

The next step down in the chain of command is the Joint Chiefs of Staff (JCS). The JCS contains the commanders of all four services: Army, Navy, Marine Corps, and Air Force. It receives the orders and recommendations of the secretary of defense and turns them into strategic goals for the armed forces. The military departments are responsible for training and equipping the armed forces and ensuring that they are ready for operations. Finally, the Unified Commands are the parts of the armed forces that actually conduct operations. A Unified Command consists of two or more services working together, usually within a designated geographical region, known as an Area of Responsibility (AOR). The AOR, for example, of the United States European Command covers 13 million square miles (34 million sq km) and 91 countries, from Norway in northern Europe, down to the Cape of Good Hope in South Africa. The U.S. Army is present in each Unified Command, and its deployments reach worldwide, from Germany to Guam.

Missions and Major Commands

If need be, U.S. Army soldiers must be prepared to go to war and risk their own lives for the preservation of U.S. values and the American way of life, as has most recently been seen in the war on terrorism in Afghanistan. However, there are many other types of missions performed by the U.S. Army. It also gives federal, state, and local government agencies military assistance when required; conducts programs of environmental protection and development; acts as a relief force in times of natural disaster (including foreign disasters); conducts humanitarian or peacekeeping operations in accordance with its U.S., NATO, or UN responsibilities; and provides emergency medical air transportation.

All of these responsibilities are conducted under the authority of the Army's Major Commands. Major Commands are the subdivisions of the Army that control all aspects of Army training and operations. Currently, there are 13 Major Commands in the U.S. Army, each with its own distinct mission and program. Here, we will look at each Major Command in turn, noting its role and jurisdiction within the U.S. Army.

U.S. Army Europe (USAREUR)

USAREUR trains, prepares, and deploys a combat-ready military force of over 50,000 troops throughout Europe, Africa, and much of the Middle East. Its missions include providing and sustaining trained and ready forces, promoting regional stability, gathering intelligence, and conducting operations and exercises in the region. USAREUR's headquarters are in Stuttgart, Germany.

The U.S. Army European Command.

U.S. Army Forces Command (FORSCOM)

FORSCOM is the U.S. Army's largest Major Command. It is actually a part of the U.S. armed forces' Atlantic Command but sends its soldiers to all worldwide destinations where they are needed. FORSCOM controls some 760,000 regular soldiers, reservists, and members of the National Guard, and it trains, mobilizes, and deploys them as required. Its headquarters are at Fort McPherson, GA.

U.S. Army Materiel Command (AMC)

The Army Materiel Command has the mission of providing the Army with the latest and best military technology available, as well as finding technological solutions to operational problems. It is headquartered in Alexandria, VA, and has over 67,000 personnel at its disposal.

The U.S. Army Materiel Command sent Army Strykers to Afghanistan. This Stryker vehicle awaits transportation to a combat area.

U.S. Army Training and Doctrine Command (TRADOC)

TRADOC takes responsibility for training U.S. Army personnel. It contains 32 military schools. TRADOC trains more than 500,000 soldiers and service members each year.

U.S. Army Corps of Engineers (USACE)

The USACE, formerly a major command and now a direct reporting unit, actually consists of approximately 37,000 civilians and soldiers. Its mission is to support the United States at home and abroad with vital engineering projects. These projects include establishing water supplies, constructing military facilities and bases, supporting other federal and defense agencies with development projects, and providing engineering response in case of national emergencies and disasters. USACE is headquartered in Washington, DC.

During a TRADOC training exercise, a team chief practices inspecting a helicopter for damage.

U.S. Army Space And Missile Defense Command/Army Forces Strategic Command (USASMDC/ARSTRAT)

USASMDC/ARSTRAT is the assigned Army Service Component Command (ASCC) to the United States Strategic Command (USSTRATCOM). Headquartered in Huntsville, AL, it provides continuous oversight, control, **integration**, and coordination of Army forces supporting USSTRATCOM.

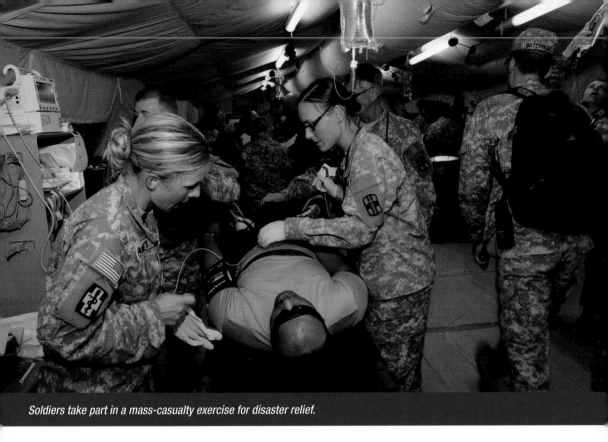

Soldiers take part in a mass-casualty exercise for disaster relief.

U.S. Army Pacific Command (USARPAC)

Formed in 1957, USARPAC contributes toward stability in the Pacific region and has strategic relations with over 41 countries, including the Philippines, Thailand, Vietnam, Japan, Mongolia, Russia, China, South Korea, India, Bangladesh, Australia, New Zealand, Marshall Islands, and Papua New Guinea. Current numbers of personnel deployed are around 38,000.

Army National Guard

The National Guard is a reserve element of the U.S. Army. It is manned mainly by civilians who act as soldiers on a part-time basis. Typical service involves the individual contributing one weekend each month and a two-week period of extended training in the summer. The National Guard fulfills both state and federal roles. The governor of a state can call upon the National Guard to assist with state emergencies, such as natural disasters, riots, or breakdowns in social order. In a federal capacity, the National Guard is used to support regular forces on peacekeeping, humanitarian, and military operations at home and abroad. The National Guard has served in recent conflicts, such as the Gulf War, and is currently being used to provide domestic protection in the war against terrorism.

U.S. Army Space and Missile Defense Command (SMDC)

The SMDC is the U.S. Army's newest Military Command, created on October 1, 1997. It implements the Army's space and national missile-defense policies, providing defense against nuclear **ballistic** missile attack and also exploring the development of space-based weapons systems.

U.S. Army South (USARSO)

A small force of around 1,800 personnel, USARSO provides support to U.S. embassies and military groups throughout Central and South America and the Caribbean. It frequently conducts humanitarian operations throughout Latin America and is headquartered in Puerto Rico.

U.S. Army North (USARNO)

Headquartered in Fort Sam Houston, TX, this command, also called The Fifth Army, contributes to a safe and secure North America. It is prepared for and resilient to natural and human made threats and hazards, resourced and postured to act decisively with domestic and international partners.

U.S. Army Cyber Command (USARCYBER)

USARCYBER directs and conducts integrated electronic warfare, with the goal of ensuring freedom of action in and through cyberspace and to deny that freedom to U.S. adversaries.

Military Surface Deployment and Distribution Command

Located at Scott Air Force Base in Illinois, this command directs transportation needs of the U.S. Army.

U.S. Army Special Operations Command (USASOC)

USASOC has the overall responsibility for recruiting, training, equipping, and deploying U.S. Army special operations personnel throughout the world. It is a very busy Major Command. During a 10-month period, for example, 23,000 USASOC soldiers deployed to 100 countries

A U.S. soldier practices firing an M4A1.

and conducted 1,600 missions. Around 10,000 Special Forces troops are trained every year at U.S. Army John F. Kennedy Special Warfare Center and School at Fort Bragg, NC.

U.S. Army Africa (USARAF)

U.S. Army Africa is headquartered in Vicenza, Italy. It conducts sustained security engagement with African land forces with the goal of promoting security, stability, and peace.

U.S. Army Central (USARCENT)

USARCENT, headquartered at Shaw Air Force Base, South Carolina, provides oversight and control of any operations throughout its jurisdiction. This includes 20 nations in the Middle East and Central and South Asia. Its goal is to protect U.S. national interests and defeat emerging threats.

The Greatest Security Force on Earth

All these commands constitute the greatest security force on Earth and keep the U.S. Army functioning smoothly. Currently in charge of this force is General Mark A. Milley, the U.S. Army chief of staff. General Milley became the 39th chief of staff in August 2015. He received his bachelor's degree from Princeton University and a master's degree in International Relations from Columbia University. He also graduated from the U.S. Naval War College and MIT's National Security Studies Program. In addition, his awards and decorations include the Defense Distinguished Service Medal; Army Distinguished Service Medal with two bronze oak leaf clusters; Defense Superior Service Medal with two bronze oak leaf clusters; Legion of Merit with two bronze oak leaf clusters, and many others.

Members of the Joint Chiefs of Staff.

General Milley occupies the highest rank in the U.S. Army, but all Army soldiers are expected to have these same character traits. Every officer and soldier within the U.S. Army commands has been trained to perform specialized and highly demanding duties. What most of them have in common is that they have all gone through the difficulties and challenges of Basic Combat Training.

Text-Dependent Questions

1. What government act and its amendments established the structure of the U.S. Army?
2. What two offices make up the National Command Authority?
3. How many major commands currently make up the U.S. Army?

Research Projects

1. Select one major command of the U.S. Army and research its role. What is its mission and what operation has it most recently performed?
2. Research the role of the U.S. Army Corps of Engineers. What is its primary function? What role do the thousands of civilians that are part of it play?

CHAPTER 3

TRAINING FOR DEFENSE

Basic training is physically rigorous and builds a range of essential military skills.

All U.S. Army soldiers have to go through Basic Combat Training, eight weeks of arduous physical and mental training. The course is tough, but it ensures that the men and women who emerge at the other end are among the best regular soldiers in the world.

U.S. Army training consists of two stages: Basic Combat Training (BCT) and Advanced Individual Training (AIT). BCT is the training program that turns new recruits into soldiers, and it is followed by AIT, which turns the soldiers into military specialists. During BCT, the much-feared drill sergeants (DSs) will be looking for individuals who can demonstrate character, endurance, and teamwork in the face of physical exhaustion and hard discipline.

The Advanced Individual Training (AIT) experience.

Basic Combat Training

Army training is conducted in any of a number of locations. The particular training school that a new recruit ends up in will usually be related to the location of the recruit's AIT. Some of the most popular destinations for BCT are Fort Knox in Louisville, KY; Fort Jackson in Columbia, SC; Fort McClellan in Anniston, AL; Fort Leonard Wood in Waynesville, MO; and Fort Still in Lawton, OK.

Words to Understand

Barracks: Building used to house soldiers.

Bayonet: Long knife attached to a rifle used in combat.

Pugil stick: Padded pole used in military training.

BCT is actually ten weeks long, but the first week is spent in what is known as the Reception Battalion. The Reception Battalion is the place where the new recruit is processed and made ready for training. This first week is quite tedious for the enthusiastic recruits. They will receive inoculations, have dental examinations, fill out official paperwork and life-insurance forms, receive their ID papers, and get their first regulation Army haircut. There are also some basic intelligence tests and a fitness test. The fitness test includes 15 push-ups, 17 sit-ups, and a 0.5-mile (0.8 km) run (to be completed in 8.5 minutes); the test varies slightly, according to the drill sergeant and the gender of the recruit. Women are not expected to complete the same number of push-ups and are given more time to complete the run.

Women of the U.S. Army in their first week the Reception Battalion.

Harshness of the Drill Instructors

Private First Class Robert Bowles gives insight into life during Basic Combat Training:

> It was common for soldiers to keep the combination on their locker already dialed in, so all they had to do was pull it open in the morning, thus saving a few seconds. Evidently, the drill sergeant had been going around searching for those troops doing that. And alas, I was the one he found.
>
> "Drill Sergeant," I said, "the private was—"
>
> "Didn't I tell you to shut up? Now you're ignoring me! Drop and give me 40 while I do a locker inspection!"
>
> I dropped to the cold, hard floor and began knocking out the push-ups as he opened my locker and grabbed my uniforms, shirts, socks, underwear, and towels and threw them down the middle of the barracks. By the time I was done with my push-ups, and had recovered to the position of attention, my locker was empty. He warned me that if I ever left one of his lockers unsecured again, he was going to throw me down the barracks aisle.

Once the Reception Battalion period is over, the recruits can look forward to the eight weeks of BCT proper. BCT is broken down into three phases: Phase I, known as Red Phase; Phase II, White Phase; and Phase III, Blue Phase.

Phase I—Red Phase

Phase I runs from Week 1 to Week 3 of BCT. Week 1 is a great shock for the recruits. They are introduced to their fearsome drill sergeant, a scowling, seemingly humorless individual who picks up on every offense against discipline, no matter how small. The recruits have to follow the drill sergeant's commands to the letter, and the typical day lasts from 4:30 a.m. to 9:00 p.m. They learn how to make beds the Army way, wear their uniforms properly, clean their **barracks** and lockers, maintain their rifle and equipment, and identify the various military ranks of the Army. Physical training also begins in earnest: lots of running (a common distance is 2 miles [3.2 km]), push-ups, sit-ups, and assault courses.

Drill sergeants are most feared in Basic Combat Training.

Week 2 continues the training. An inspection is made of the recruits' living space, locker, rifle, and equipment. Every fault receives a sharp reprimand or punishment. The trainees will receive instruction in parade-ground drill and ceremonies, but they will also have their first combat training, learning some of the basics of **bayonet** fighting and combat first aid. They have a detailed introduction to their gun, the M16A2 rifle.

M16A2 rifle qualification.

A distinctive exercise of Week 2 (sometimes Week 3) is the "Gas Chamber." This is a room filled with CS gas. Recruits have to step inside, then twice remove their respirator to recount their name, rank, and social security number. Most recruits emerge with eyes stinging and full of tears; many are also vomiting.

U.S. Army tear gas training.

Week 3 builds up the physical exercise and combat training and includes sparring with **pugil sticks**, unarmed combat training, and land navigation instruction.

Phase II—White Phase

White Phase lasts for Weeks 4–6. Week 4 takes the recruits to the firing ranges, where they learn to use the M16A2 rifle, shooting at a variety of moving, pop-up, and long-range targets. Soon they progress to hand grenades. At first, only dummy grenades are thrown, then each recruit gets to throw fragmentation grenades.

Week 5 increases the demands of M16 marksmanship, and the recruit will practice automatic fire and night firing. The recruit needs to hit at least 17 out of 40 targets to pass as a "marksman," but a strike rate of more than 24 will earn a "sharpshooter" badge. Physical training focuses on combat-type assault courses. The recruits have to run around the obstacle course in full kit. **Live** machine-gun fire will sometimes be directed over their heads, or small **pyrotechnics** charges will be detonated nearby to increase the impression of combat. To compensate for this trauma, the recruits will then be introduced to firing light antitank weapons, like the light antitank weapon (LAW) rocket, a portable, shoulder-fired rocket.

Week 6 raises the physical demands. In full kit, recruits will have to negotiate eight-mile (13 km) speed-marches and perform well in the many physical exercises. At this stage, many recruits notice that they are starting to think, behave, and perform more like soldiers. Whether this is actually true or not is tested in Phase III.

Soldiers practice firing the XM8, a lightweight assault rifle.

Phase III—Blue Phase

Blue Phase tests the military skills and physical strength that the recruits should have picked up over the previous six weeks. During Week 7, the recruits take their final Army Physical Fitness Test (APFT). They must score at least 150 points to pass this, but by this stage, most do so without too much trouble.

After this, the recruits embark on a one-week period of full-blown military exercises, which include digging foxholes, deploying ambushes and patrols, and showing their abilities to communicate effectively and respond to crises. If they can come through this end-of-cycle test, they will be classified as U.S. Army soldiers. After spending most of Week 8 in preparation, they will then attend a formal graduation ceremony.

The end of Basic Combat Training marks a new beginning for hundreds of new soldiers.

Advanced Individual Training and Officer Training

U.S. Army basic training.

AIT is an extension of BCT and teaches soldiers their Military Occupational Specialty (MOS). The MOS training programs vary greatly, depending on what profession the soldier pursues within the Army—there are over 400 different types of jobs within the U.S. armed forces for a soldier to do. A soldier could go on to become a tank gunner, an airborne soldier, a helicopter pilot, an artillery gunner, or an intelligence operative. Often, the AIT is conducted at the same place as the BCT, and the typical soldier may undergo about 13 weeks of training from the beginning of the BCT to the end of the AIT.

Officers are recruited into the Army from several sources, chiefly the Reserve Officers' Training Corps (ROTC) at various universities and colleges throughout the United States; the Officer Candidate School at Fort Benning, GA; and prestigious institutions, like the U.S. Military Academy at West Point. Standard training to be a U.S. Army officer can last up to a year. In institutions like West Point, where the cadets also take baccalaureate degrees over a four-year course, only 1,300 soldiers pass out of about 14,000 applicants each year. Officers undergo the same BCT as regular soldiers, although they often have to show more advanced physical fitness. They also have to demonstrate the qualities of leadership and character necessary to inspire soldiers in battle.

Whether training officers or regular soldiers, the U.S. Army consistently produces superb troops, well versed in the arts of war.

Text-Dependent Questions

1. What is the difference between Basic Combat Training and Advanced Individual Training?
2. What times does a typical day begin and end during the first three weeks of Basic Combat Training?
3. What strike rate does a recruit need to have to earn the title of sharp-shooter?

Research Projects

1. Research the ROTC How do people join the organization and how many of these become officers in the U.S. Army?
2. Research West Point Military Academy. How many applicants are accepted? How many graduates go on to become officers in the U.S. Army?

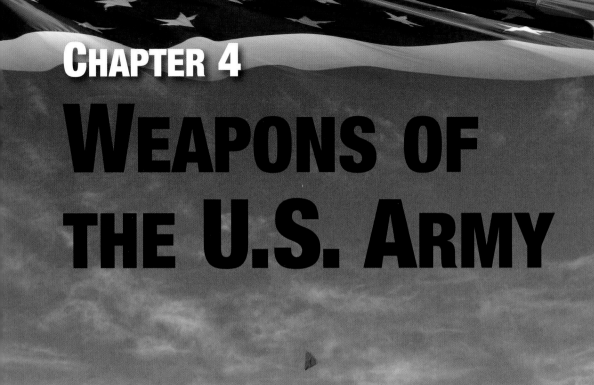

CHAPTER 4

WEAPONS OF THE U.S. ARMY

The U.S. Army's Tactical Missile System, shown above, has fired almost 600 missiles in combat in more than 25 years of deployment.

No other army in the world comes close to the power of the U.S. Army's weapons systems. The U.S. defense industry has kept the army at the cutting edge of military technology, knowing that the future defense of the United States depends on it.

On February 4, 1991, during the Gulf War, the Allied forces launched a massive assault from Saudi Arabia into neighboring Kuwait and Iraq. Their goal was to push the occupying Iraqi forces out of Kuwait and back into Iraq. They faced nearly half a million Iraqi troops and a massive force of enemy tanks, mainly Soviet-era T-62s and T-72s. The T-72, in particular, was well able to destroy a tank at distances of over two miles (3.2 km) with its advanced antiarmor ammunition. However, they were up against nearly 1,900 U.S. Army M1A1 Abrams tanks, one of the most advanced tanks in the world.

When the tank armies finally clashed, the Iraqis were totally outclassed. The Abrams is capable of firing accurately even while on the move over rough ground, and its advanced 120-millimeter (mm) smooth-bore Rheinmetall gun outranged the Iraqi firepower by over 3,048 feet (1,000 m). Using Forward-Looking InfraRed (FLIR) technology, the crews could also see all the Iraqi vehicles, even in the darkness of night or through the smoke and dust of desert battle. In total, the Iraqis lost 3,847 tanks during the war; no U.S. tanks were lost to Iraqi armor.

This battle illustrates why technology can be decisive in conflict. The U.S. Army spends over $30 billion each year on developing new equipment for waging war. It would be impossible to list the many different types of weaponry in the U.S. arsenal, but we can look at some of the individual weapons that contribute to the Army's technological superiority on any battlefield.

Words to Understand

Firepower: Strength of weapons.

Monocle: Single round lens worn in one eye.

Quash: Stop completely.

M1A2 Abrams Main Battle Tank

We have already seen the capabilities of the M1A1 Abrams tank. The latest U.S. tank is the M1A2 upgrade of the Abrams, and it represents the best of worldwide tank technology. The basic MI Abrams tank weighs 120,249 lbs. (54,545 kg) and has a maximum road speed of 44 mph (72 km/h). It is armed with one 105 mm main gun, two 7.62 mm machine guns, one .50-caliber machine gun, and six smoke-grenade launchers. It has day and night fire-on-the-move capability; a laser range finder, to give the precise distance to a target; a thermal-imaging night sight; optical day sight; and a digital ballistic computer, to calculate the precise targeting of the gun, allowing for wind, distance, and the movement of the enemy vehicle. Its armor type is classified, but it can stop most antitank shells. The Abrams can also be fitted with explosive reactive armor. This armor has an explosive filling that, when struck by an enemy shell, explodes outward and thus cancels the force of the explosion against it.

The basic M1 is a superb machine, but it is far surpassed by the M1A2. The M1A2 has a new FLIR targeting system for its 120 mm gun, which gives a 70 percent improvement in finding the target, 45 percent improvement in the speed of fire, 30 percent greater range, and enhanced accuracy. A Thermal Management System (TMS) keeps the temperature inside the tank below 95°F (35°C), whatever the combat conditions.

Although other nations have advanced tanks, such as the British Challenger II and the French Le Clerc, the M1A2 Abrams is recognized as one of the best tanks in the world today.

An M1A2 Abrams tank with urban warfare upgrade.

AH-64 Apache

The U.S. Army has a large fleet of aircraft, both fixed-wing (airplanes) and rotary-wing (helicopters). Its fixed-wing fleet is largely concerned with transportation and uses aircraft such as the C-130 Hercules and C-23 Sherpa. However, it is the rotary-wing aircraft that have now become the most influential combat aircraft in the U.S. Army. The Army created the concept of the helicopter gunship back in the Vietnam War, and several decades later, it has produced the ultimate war machine, the AH-64 Apache.

The Apache entered service in 1984, having been developed by McDonnell Douglas (now Boeing). More than 800 Apaches are currently in service with the Army. They were used to great effect during the Gulf War, when entire Iraqi columns of armored vehicles were destroyed by Apaches hovering many miles away, out of visual range, but within weapons range.

The Apache is a twin-engined attack helicopter. Its **firepower** is awesome. It carries a 30 mm Boeing M230 chain gun under its nose, which is capable of firing 625 explosive cannon shells per minute. Antiarmor capability is provided by 16 Lockheed Martin/Boeing AGM-114D Longbow Hellfire air-to-surface missiles. These have a maximum range of 7.4 miles (12 km) and work in "fire-and-forget" mode—in other words, once released they guide themselves to the target without the assistance of the helicopter crew. Using the millimeter-wave Longbow seeker radar, the Hellfires can be launched even though the crew cannot see their target. From spotting a target to launching a missile can take as little as 30 seconds, and its onboard computers can track, monitor, and target up to 265 separate targets at once. Other weapons include four Sidewinder air-to-air missiles for defense against enemy aircraft; and pods of 2.75-inch (69.85 mm) rockets for use against area targets. All information derived from the target-acquisition system is visually presented in the monocular eyepiece of the Honeywell Integrated Helmet and Display Sighting System (IHADSS) worn by the pilot and copilot. Apaches will remain at the vanguard of U.S. Army operations for the foreseeable future, and over 1,000 have been exported to countries abroad who want to benefit from the Apache's amazing versatility and firepower.

An AH-64D Apache Longbow helicopter.

Multiple Launch Rocket System (MLRS)

While the U.S. Army has many fine artillery pieces in its arsenal, the single most devastating is the MLRS M270. This is not a gun, but a mobile rocket-launcher system. The launcher vehicle carries 12 rocket tubes. The tubes can be loaded and fired in a ripple pattern in only five minutes, and each high-explosive or cluster-bomb rocket has a range of up to 31 miles (50 km), although the Army TACMS Block IA missile can reach up to 186 miles (300 km). The effect on the target is devastating. One Iraqi officer in the Gulf War told how his unit was reduced from 600 men to only 175 after a single strike by the MLRS. Each rocket can be programmed to

A view of an MLRS self-propelled launcher loader (right).

explode just above the ground, so that the enemy has little chance to find shelter, and M77 warheads split into 644 small, individual bombs that either explode immediately or detonate some time later. Another warhead, the AT2, disperses 28 antitank mines over the target area. The latest MLRS features an Improved Fire Control System (IFCS), which uses the Global Positioning System (GPS) to put down rockets within a few yards of the target.

Future Warriors

The Abrams tank, the Apache, and the MLRS are just three examples of the war-winning technologies that protect the United States. There are many more. The individual soldier in the U.S. Army has never been better armed, and there is no army on Earth that comes close to matching U.S. Army firepower.

So what of the future? One of the most important developments for the individual soldier is the Land Warrior Project. Land Warrior is a 10 lb (4.5 kg) portable laptop computer built into the soldier's uniform. The computer is linked to a head-mounted display (HMD) **monocle** worn over the left eye, through which the soldier sees a digitized plan of the battlefield and receives a stream of tactical information, including the geophysical contours ahead, the position of all unit members, the position of enemy forces, enemy weaponry information, large-scale maps of the area, the soldier's location via GPS, and logistics information.

A U.S. Army soldier showcasing the elements of the Land Warrior System.

All about the Land Warrior System.

The computer console is worn on the chest with a flip-down screen, the mouse being located on the soldier's rifle, and can be used silently to send emails and operational data between soldiers and backup forces. To improve efficiency, laser sensors and thermal-imaging systems on the rifle—which are connected to the computer—enable the soldier to target an enemy accurately at night or in zero visibility, and even to aim the weapon around corners without breaking cover at all.

Objective Individual Combat Weapon

At present, the U.S. Army uses the M16A2 rifle as its standard infantry firearm. However, over the next 10 years, more and more M16s are likely to be replaced by the Objective Individual Combat Weapon (OICW). The OICW is the ultimate in futuristic firepower. It has two main weapons: a 0.21-inch (5.56 mm) assault rifle and a 0.5-inch (20 mm) grenade launcher. Both weapons use a computerized infrared electronic aiming system, which allows targeting even at night and through smoke. The grenade launcher is also fitted with a laser range-finder. This fires out a laser beam that tells the ammunition in the weapon the exact distance to the target. When the grenade is fired, it is programmed to explode in the air directly above the target. Even an enemy hiding behind a wall is not safe from such a weapon.

Land Warrior is a glimpse into the future of war, but it is a future that will come soon. The U.S. Army will work hard to make sure that its technology is always the best possible to help its soldiers survive battles and to **quash** the tactics of any enemy.

Text-Dependent Questions

1. What was the goal of the Allied Forces assault on February 4, 1991, during the Gulf War?
2. How does the M1A2 Abrams tank protect occupants from enemy shell fire?
3. What benefit does a Hellfire Longbow missile give to its users?

Research Projects

1. Research the M1A2 Abrams tank. How many are operational in the U.S Army today, and where are they deployed?
2. Research the AH-64 Apache helicopter. How many are operational in the U.S Army today, and where are they deployed?

CHAPTER 5

CHEMICAL, NUCLEAR, AND BIOLOGICAL DEFENSE

Modern soldiers receive special training in using protective gear.

The attacks of September 11, 2001, and the subsequent anthrax attacks via the U.S. mail system awoke America to the possible threats from what are known as weapons of mass destruction (WMDs).

WMDs are chemical, biological, or nuclear devices that are capable of killing more than 5,000 people in a single deployment. Though the **anthrax** attacks did not achieve a large death toll, the disruption to daily life was enormous. Fortunately, however, the U.S. Army is prepared to meet the challenge of further WMD attacks with two of its own special departments: the U.S. Army Space and Missile Defense Command (SMDC) and the U.S. Army Soldier and Biological Chemical Command (SBCCOM).

U.S. Army Space and Missile Defense Command (SMDC)

Although the United States has played its part in reducing the amount of nuclear weapons in the world, many more countries have acquired nuclear capabilities over the last 20 years. China now has the Dong Feng series of Intercontinental Ballistic Missiles (ICBMs), including the Dong Feng 31. This can deliver a single 2.5-megaton nuclear warhead (equivalent to 2.5 millions tons of dynamite being exploded) or three 90-kiloton warheads (90,000 tons of dynamite) up to a range of 7,500 miles (12,065 km)—far enough to reach the United States. China is not the only country to develop nuclear capabilities. Both India and Pakistan, traditionally great enemies of each other, have nuclear arsenals. Iraq is believed to be attempting to develop nuclear weapons. Communist North Korea has also been developing a nuclear **arsenal** since 1947. Weapons

Words to Understand

Anthrax: Serious disease that affects animals and sometimes people.

Arsenal: A collection of weapons.

Scud: Missile first used by the U.S.S.R.

analysts estimate that North Korea has somewhere between 10 and 25 nuclear weapons, and the country has conducted five successful tests of its nuclear weapons since 2006.

SMDC is the part of the U.S. Army that combats this nuclear threat. It is a Major Command and focuses on exploiting space for military purposes and producing the technology to protect the United States from nuclear attack. SMDC is the newest of the Major Commands, created on October 1, 1997. However, the Army has been responsible for ballistic missile defense since the 1950s. In 1962, the Army used a Nike-Zeus missile to successfully intercept a test ballistic missile during its flight.

Today, SMDC has a sophisticated range of earthbound and space-based technologies either ready for action or in development. Three in particular are worth mentioning: the Patriot Advanced Capability-3 (PAC-3), the Theater High Altitude Area Defense (THAAD), and the Space-Based Laser (SBL).

The PAC-3 is a high-velocity, surface-to-air missile that can hit incoming ballistic missiles and destroy their high-explosive, biological, chemical, or nuclear warheads. It actively seeks out the enemy missile, climbing to an altitude of 78,750 feet (24,000 m) in a matter of

A Patriot Advanced Capability-3 missile launches during a target test.

seconds before exploding in the attacking missile's vicinity. It has a range of 37 miles (60 km). Patriots were used in action in the Gulf War to down Iraqi **Scud** missiles fired at Israel. Since then, major improvements have been made to increase their accuracy, speed, and knock-down power. Patriots are often part of the THAAD system.

THAAD consists of the rocket launcher, plus the THAAD radar system and the THAAD battle management/command, control, communications, and intelligence (BM/C3I) system. The THAAD's radar technology tracks all incoming missiles, then targets them and releases a Patriot or similar missile in seconds, tracking the missile to target while it is in flight. The full THAAD system began operation in 2008.

The SBL is the future of the Army's missile-defense program. Special combat satellites will orbit Earth armed with high-powered laser beams. The satellites will be able to detect any ballistic missile at the very moment it is launched—wherever on the globe it is launched from—then track it and attack it with lasers until the missile is destroyed. SBL technology is still being researched, and no current target date for its use has been published. With a network

This THAAD missile carries no warhead but relies on the force of the impact to destroy the incoming missile.

of such weapons orbiting Earth, the U.S. Army could provide an almost impenetrable shield of protection over the United States against missile attacks.

Dangers from Anthrax

Following the September 11, 2001, attacks on America, the U.S. suffered a series of biological attacks using the bacteria anthrax. Anthrax is the disease produced by the bacteria *Bacillus* anthracis. It is a lethal disease and one particularly useful for terrorist use since it is easy to manufacture, can be spread over a wide area, and can be stored for a long time. There are three types of anthrax: cutaneous anthrax—infection through the skin or via a cut; gastrointestinal anthrax—infection through eating anthrax-contaminated foods; and inhalation anthrax—infection through inhaling anthrax spores. The last type is by far the most dangerous. The symptoms begin with a flulike illness followed by severe difficulty breathing, internal bleeding, and, ultimately, respiratory collapse. Thankfully, there were few deaths from inhalation anthrax following the 2001 attacks, and U.S. Army and civilian disease-control scientists have been developing antidotes and vaccines to combat this terrible threat. As of 2016, no antidote was in use, although one had worked well on animals by 2013.

U.S. Army Soldier and Biological Chemical Command (SBCCOM)

Chemical and biological weapons are some of the most frightening WMDs. Several countries hostile to the United States have biological and chemical warfare capabilities. Iraq, for instance, has the lethal agents anthrax, botulinum toxin, ricin, and aflatoxin, and is also developing at least 34 other agents for use in warfare.

SBCCOM's role is to guard the United States against these threats. Its mission states the following: "Develop, integrate, acquire, and sustain soldier and NBC defense technology, systems, and services to ensure the decisive edge and maximum protection for the United States." In addition to developing or disposing of chemical and biological weapons, SBCCOM is involved with preparing the U.S. Army to deal effectively with any WMD attack within U.S. shores. It has its own rapid-response force—the Army Technical Escort Unit. This highly trained chemical/biological response team has over 50 years of experience in handling chemical and biological threats and materials.

SBCCOM has a vital role in preparing U.S. soldiers for chemical and biological warfare, developing the protective suits, detection tools, and decontamination equipment that will enable the Army to keep functioning in even the most hostile chemical and biological environment. It is also involved in the federal Domestic Preparedness Program (DPP). The DPP sends SBCCOM personnel out into U.S. communities to train local civilian, emergency, and law enforcement agencies in dealing with chemical and biological incidents. More than 105 communities have received special training.

Scientists from the U.S. Army Edgewood Chemical Biological Center test for chemical war agents in munitions.

Text-Dependent Questions

1. Name two or more countries that are thought to have an arsenal of nuclear weapons.
2. What is the range of the PAC-3 missile?
3. Name three lethal biological agents used in warfare.

Research Projects

1. Research the community training provided by the DPP. What are agencies trained to do and what will their role be in an emergency?
2. Research proposed SBL technologies? Which is most likely to be deployed and by what date?

CHAPTER 6
FIGHTING FOR FREEDOM ABROAD

More than 9,300 American soldiers are interred in the Normandy American Cemetery and Memorial, created after the successful D-Day operation that began the liberation of Europe in World War II.

The U.S. Army is not only committed to homeland defense. As part of the United States' ongoing attempts to make the world more peaceable and democratic, the army is constantly deployed across the world in the causes of freedom and humanitarian aid.

Since World War II, the roles of the U.S. Army have changed tremendously. It still has its traditional duty of fighting, of course: during the last 50 years, the Army has fought in major wars, including the Korean War (1950–1952), the Vietnam War (1963–1975), the Gulf War (1990–1991), and, at present, the war against terrorism in Afghanistan (2001–). Yet this type of operation is only part of what the Army accomplishes; its work also includes what are known as operations other than war (OOTWs). OOTWs include delivering humanitarian relief, acting as peacekeeping troops in foreign war zones, providing engineering support in poor countries, combating drug trafficking, and apprehending foreign warlords.

This demanding breadth of operations takes the U.S. Army all over the world; the soldiers trying also to promote social harmony and democratic values. For example, in Africa alone, the U.S. Army is performing the following tasks:

U.S. Army explosive-**ordnance** disposal experts have been deployed to Nigeria, central Africa, to help local military forces clear away unexploded bombs and mines left over from its civil war.

- Soldiers from the U.S. Army Corps of Engineers are helping to build flood defenses in the countries of Mozambique, Botswana, South Africa, and Zimbabwe as part of Operation Atlas Response.

Words to Understand

Convoy: To travel with and protect someone or something.

Humanitarian: Agency or person working for social reform or betterment.

Ordnance: Military supplies.

- U.S. Army troops have built a 430,520-square-foot (40,000 sq m) aid center in Gabon, which will be used to store aid materials and can also house refugees in times of disaster.
- As part of the African Crisis Response Initiative, U.S. Army soldiers train African troops in the techniques of humanitarian and peacekeeping work, including convoy protection, food distribution, and the treating of refugees. Similar work is being conducted around the world in regions such as southern Europe, Latin America, and the Far East, as well as homeland U.S. territories. These operations often go unreported by the world's media.
- OOTWs form a large part of the U.S. Army's worldwide commitment. Unfortunately, however, operations involving combat are all too regular. Many U.S. soldiers have sacrificed their lives in action since World War II, defending against tyranny and oppression in various forms. Between 1950 and 1952, the U.S. Army formed a large part of the United Nations army fighting Communist North Korea, which was attempting to take over democratic South Korea. Similarly, U.S. ground troops in 1963–1973 fought in the defense of South Vietnam against Communist North Vietnam in the Vietnam War. The Gulf War was concerned with ejecting Iraqi forces from their occupation of neighboring Kuwait. U.S. forces in the former Yugoslavia, Europe, were deployed in the 1990s to prevent the massacre and displacement of millions of local people. In all these cases, the U.S. Army was sent to defend peoples whom the world could well have abandoned to their fate.

We will now look at two of the landmark operations of the last 30 years, both involving the U.S. Army's elite Rangers, and we will see what lessons the Army has learned.

Grenada, 1983

On October 19, 1983, the government of Grenada (an island in the Caribbean) was overthrown in a bloody act of revolution. The new government was hard-line Communist, and the safety of over 1,000 U.S. medical students and their families on the island was in jeopardy. The Organization of Eastern Caribbean States requested that the United States make a military intervention, and the U.S. government quickly agreed.

Time was of the essence. A large U.S. Army, Navy, and Air Force operation was quickly put together and launched on October 25. The key to the operation, named Operation Urgent Fury, was the swift capture of the Port Salinas airfield, thus enabling U.S. troops to be landed and from there to advance to the True Blue Medical Campus to rescue the U.S. citizens, and then to gain further security by capturing the Cuban army camp at Calivigny. U.S. Army Rangers prepared for dramatic action. They planned to launch their action from C-130 aircraft, which were to land on the airstrip. However, when the operation was launched, it was found that the airstrip had been covered in obstacles. Within 15 minutes, the Rangers had prepared themselves for a parachute jump.

A U.S. Army Bell AH-1S Cobra helicopter fires its cannon.

At 6:30 a.m., the Rangers began their jump. They immediately met resistance, but by 10 a.m., the Rangers had quashed enemy fire and cleared the runway for reinforcements and equipment to be flown in. The Rangers quickly advanced to the True Blue Campus, and the U.S. students were taken unharmed to the airfield and evacuated. The only disaster of the operation occurred when three Black Hawk helicopters crashed during the assault on the Calivigny army base, in which three Rangers died.

Despite Operation Urgent Fury revealing several problems in U.S. military operations, it had been a success. All U.S. citizens were rescued from the island, and total U.S. casualties were 19 dead and 152 wounded. The Rangers, in particular, had demonstrated their capability as one of the U.S. Army's top units.

Mogadishu, Somalia, 1993

The battle in Mogadishu—capital of the African country Somalia—took place in October 1993 and has gone down in history as one of the most dramatic U.S. Army actions since World War II. It was immortalized in the Hollywood movie *Black Hawk Down.*

In 1993, U.S. Army troops were stationed in Somalia, performing humanitarian roles. The troops of a local warlord, Mohammed Farah Aidid, were responsible for much of the continuing violence around the capital, Mogadishu. It was eventually decided that Aidid had to be removed to stabilize the situation. At 3:30 p.m. on October 3, 1993, U.S. Black Hawk helicopters took off, carrying a large assault team of U.S. Rangers and Delta Force operatives. They were heading for the Olympic Hotel in the center of Mogadishu, where Aidid was supposed to be meeting his lieutenants. The mission was to launch a surprise assault against the hotel, capture Aidid, and bring him to justice.

From the first moment that U.S. troops touched down, however, nothing went according to plan. Hundreds of civilians, all armed with Kalashnikov rifles and rocket-propelled grenades, opened fire on the Ranger team. While the Rangers established a perimeter around the hotel, the Delta team went inside, but found no Aidid. They did take 20 prisoners, who were loaded onto a **convoy** of U.S. Army vehicles that had followed the air units into the city. From this moment on, it seemed like all hell had broken loose.

A reenactment of the Battle of Mogadishu in Somalia.

The true story of *Black Hawk Down.*

At 4:20 p.m., a Black Hawk helicopter was shot down by a rocket-propelled grenade five blocks from the hotel. A Ranger unit set off to rescue the crew but came under blistering fire all the way. Every doorway and window seemed to hold an enemy weapon spraying fire. Even women and children were armed with Kalashnikovs. At 4.40 p.m., another Black Hawk was downed, and two Delta Force soldiers died trying to save the copilot. The convoy with the prisoners attempted to get back to base but was hindered by a terrifying wall of bullets and rockets. Eventually, it escaped, but 90 Rangers were left behind in the hostile city.

Darkness fell. The Rangers inside Mogadishu fought throughout the night and set up a medical treatment center to treat the many wounded. Little Bird helicopters dropped fresh ammunition and attacked the Somali gunmen, but the situation became increasingly desperate. Back at the base, General Montgomery, the commander of the mission, sent out a rescue convoy. It was beaten back by heavy fire in the narrow streets. Eventually, local Malaysian and Pakistani UN forces lent the U.S. convoy some tanks, and a 70-vehicle fighting convoy eventually broke through to the beleaguered Rangers. At 5:20 a.m. on

Black Hawk helicopters prepare to touch down during Operation Urgent Fury.

October 4, the trapped Rangers and the surviving helicopter crew were loaded aboard the convoy. The vehicles were so full that some Rangers had to run out of the city alongside the convoy while under streams of enemy fire. Finally, they made it back to their base in a sports stadium.

Eighteen U.S. soldiers died and 84 were wounded in Mogadishu. The operation had taught the U.S. Army in the harshest possible fashion about the dangers of **humanitarian** work in dangerous lands. Since Mogadishu, the U.S. Army has been more cautious about the situations into which it sends its soldiers. Yet humanitarian work around the world continues, and the bravery of the soldiers who fought in the battle is an inspiration to all U.S. Army personnel. Two soldiers killed in the fighting received the Congressional Medal of Honor, the highest military decoration in the United States.

Grenada and Mogadishu both demonstrate that U.S. soldiers abroad frequently risk their lives for the health, freedom, and peace of others. They are also engaged in defending the United States against the tyranny of terrorism, the subject of the next chapter.

Text-Dependent Questions

1. What does the acronym OOTWs stand for?
2. How has the U.S. Army Corps of Engineers helped African countries?
3. Describe the U.S. Army's role in the battle at Mogadishu, Somalia, in Africa.

Research Projects

1. Research Operation Urgent Fury. How many U.S. Army troops were involved and what was their role in the operation?
2. Research the movie *Black Hawk Down*. Was it an accurate portrayal of the Battle of Mogadishu? How was it different from actual events? How was it the same?

CHAPTER 7

THE WAR AGAINST TERRORISM

Clouds of smoke rise from fires at the World Trade Center Towers as a result of terrorist attack on September 11, 2001. Photographed 9:54 a.m. in lower Manhattan.

Since September 11, 2001, the United States has been fighting a new war—a war against terrorism. The U.S. Army has put all its resources into this fight and is already beginning to defeat global terrorist organizations using its elite troops.

On September 11, 2001, at 8:45 a.m., American Airlines Flight 11, carrying 81 passengers and 11 crew, smashed into the north tower of the World Trade Center in New York City. Twenty minutes later, United Airlines Flight 175, with 56 passengers and nine crew, hit the south tower. Both towers eventually collapsed from the devastation of the subsequent fire. Approximately half an hour after the second crash, American Airlines Flight 77 took off from Dulles International Airport (outside Washington, DC), bound for Los Angeles. Shortly after takeoff, it plowed into the Pentagon building. Thirty minutes later, United Flight 93, from Newark, NJ, to San Francisco, crashed near Shanksville, PA, killing all 38 passengers and seven crew. The combined death toll from all these incidents exceeded 3,000 people. While the first crash seemed like a nightmarish accident, the subsequent crashes soon made it clear that the United States was under a terrorist attack of unimaginable proportions. The country has changed irrevocably since the attacks. No longer can it believe itself immune from world terrorism. While the rest of the world has been experiencing terrorist attacks since the 1950s, the United States has been mainly free from such incidents.

Words to Understand

Insurgent: Person or group opposing a government or authority.

Mortars: A cannon or similar firing device.

Sabotage: Deliberately destroying something so it can't be used.

President George W. Bush quickly rose to the challenge of the new situation and declared a "war on terrorism," promising that any terrorist group around the world would be flushed out and destroyed. The U.S. Army has been at the vanguard of this fight, particularly through the use of its special forces, which are uniquely trained to combat terrorists and **insurgents.** The prime suspect for the attacks is the Al Qaeda network, a radical Islamic organization with units, bases, and operatives throughout the Middle East, but particularly concentrated in Afghanistan.

Afghanistan was the base of Al Qaeda's leader, Osama bin Laden, who was seen on video after the attacks, boasting about his planning of them. Previously, in February 1998, he had said that it was the duty of all Muslims to kill U.S. citizens. Sadly, some believed him.

Al Qaeda were protected in Afghanistan by a regime known as the Taliban. The Taliban imposed merciless and cruel leadership; under their harsh interpretation of Islamic law, women were beaten for even showing their faces. Afghanistan is one of the poorest countries on Earth, and the Taliban made the lives of already desperate people even worse. It was evident in the United States that the fight against terrorism meant overthrowing the Taliban, finding and capturing or killing Osama bin Laden, and then rooting out all terrorist networks across the world. It was time for the U.S. Army to go into action.

Post–September 11 Attacks

After Osama Bin Laden was killed by U.S. forces under President Obama in 2011, terrorism and attacks against countries in Europe and the United States did not end. From the remnants of Al Qaeda in Iraq, a new organization formed, called the Islamic State. It formed in 2013 and became known as ISIS. It is led by Abu Bakr al-Baghdadi. The organization has claimed credit for many terrorist attacks against European countries, such as Belgium, France, Canada, Turkey, the United States, and Germany, as well as many Middle Eastern countries. The U.S. Army Special Forces has worked with Iraq's Golden Division to help hold ground against ISIS and play a frontline role in the ongoing war in Iraq.

U.S. Army Special Operations Forces

On October 21, 2001, the U.S. Joint Chiefs of Staff confirmed that U.S. Army special forces and elite Rangers were engaged in pitched battles with the Taliban inside Afghanistan. The first battles took place at Al Qaeda's spiritual stronghold of Kandahar, in the southeast of the country, and at an airfield 60 miles (96 km) away. U.S. Rangers took the airfield in a ferocious, 30-minute gun battle, while special forces soldiers assisted friendly Afghan units, known as the Northern Alliance, in taking Kandahar. On December 7, Kandahar fell to the Allies.

U.S. Special Forces have been in action in Afghanistan continuously since late October 2001, alongside other elite forces, including the British Special Air Service (SAS). Much about their op-

A U.S. Army Special Operations sniper.

erations is not known, because these elite troops value their anonymity and operational privacy. So what do we know of the U.S. Special Forces soldiers, and how will they fight terrorism?

U.S. Army Special Operations Forces (SOF) soldiers come under the jurisdiction of the U.S. Army Special Operations Command. The soldiers under its command fall into the following categories:

- **Special Forces Groups (SFGs)**
- **Rangers**
- **Special Operations Aviation**
- **Psychological Operations**
- **Civil Affairs**
- **Signal and Combat Service Support**

They also include the counterterrorism unit Delta Force, more accurately known as Special Forces Operational Detachment Delta. Delta Force is a distinct part of the special forces. Usually, Special Forces units are organized according to Operational Detachments A and B. Often, five "A teams" will be commanded by one "B team." The main combat groups are described next.

Operation Anaconda

In March 2002, U.S. SOF were engaged in Operation Anaconda, named after the snake that slowly constricts its prey to death. It was involved in heavy fighting with Al Qaeda and Taliban terrorists around Gardez in the mountainous eastern region of Afghanistan. The operation began when U.S. aircraft dropped more than 450 bombs on suspected enemy positions. SOF troops and soldiers from the 101st Airborne and 10th Mountain divisions were then helicoptered into the region and immediately faced heavy resistance. One unit of the 10th Mountain Division fought a 20-hour gun battle with the enemy. An MH-47 Chinook helicopter was hit by a rocket-propelled grenade (RPG), and another MH-47 was also shot down. These incidents resulted in the deaths of seven U.S. soldiers, and another soldier was killed in a firefight with Al Qaeda rebels.

However, the losses to the Afghan opponents numbered in the hundreds. U.S. SOF troops blasted out Al Qaeda fighters from their mountainous positions using antitank rockets, and also captured mortars, RPGs, rifles, and ammunition. The Taliban and Al Qaeda fighters were forced to withdraw.

Commenting on the action, President Bush remarked: "I'm obviously saddened by the loss of life. On the other hand, I think most Americans . . . understand the cause is important and the cause is just. Our country is still under threat and so long as our country is under threat, this great nation will hunt down those who want to harm innocent Americans."

Special Forces Groups

There are currently eight known SFGs, with approximately 1,400 men in each group—women are currently not allowed to join the special forces. According to official SOF publicity, "The mission of the Special Forces Groups is to plan, prepare for, and when directed, deploy to conduct unconventional warfare, foreign internal defense, special reconnaissance, and direct actions in support of U.S. national policy objectives within designated areas of responsibility."

Rangers

The U.S. Army Rangers are a large formation of elite infantry. Their main role is to capture key terrain or destroy enemy positions in hostile environments, often in places well beyond large-scale Army support. The Rangers are specialists in airborne and mountain warfare, making them ideal for missions in places like Afghanistan.

U.S. Army Rangers at a training exercise.

160th Special Operations Aviation Regiment

This is a unique unit of pilots trained to deploy or extract SOF soldiers during missions behind enemy lines. They also conduct reconnaissance missions and, in certain circumstances, combat air strikes.

Delta Force differs slightly from the others. It was created in the late 1970s under the authorization of ex-President Jimmy Carter. While the countries of Europe had already established their own counterterrorist organizations, the United States lagged behind, mainly because the U.S. mainland did not suffer from terrorist attacks. Delta Force was created in 1977 to plug this gap by the former SOF commander Colonel Charles Beckwith. Since its foundation, Delta Force has fought in many wars and actions, including deployments in the Gulf War, Somalia, and the former Yugoslavia.

U.S. Special Forces are among the most highly trained soldiers in the world. All SOF recruits must already be serving as soldiers with exemplary records of service. The SOF training program lasts up to a year, and during that time, about 80 percent of the recruits will fail the course. Would-be Rangers attend the demanding Ranger school, while SOF recruits go to John F. Kennedy Special Warfare Center in Fort Bragg, NC. Because he was fascinated by unconventional warfare, President Kennedy was the force behind the creation of the original 5th Special Forces Group in Vietnam in the 1960s.

During SOF training, recruits will be put through physical tests that push their endurance to the limit, but they will also learn skills not taught to the regular soldier. These skills include engineering, foreign languages, medicine, intelligence gathering, **sabotage**, demolitions, advanced communications, survival, and escape and evasion.

Those soldiers that do pass recruitment are ideally suited to counterterrorist warfare. They can act alone in isolated places, regardless of the terrain or weather. When a terrorist base is identified, they can hit it hard with maximum firepower. SOF snipers can take out terrorist leaders from distances of more than 3,048 ft (1,000 m). They can also track down terrorists using expert tracking and surveillance skills.

An MH-60 Black Hawk with the Special Operations Aviation Regiment provides air support for Army Rangers.

Such are the qualities currently being used in Afghanistan, and which will be used throughout the world in the battle against terrorism. At home, 7,685 reservist soldiers were brought into active service to protect the U.S. homeland as part of Operation Noble Eagle. These soldiers are currently guarding important places.

The U.S. Army soldier is part of an elite group that will be relentless in its war against terrorism. The road ahead will undoubtedly be hard, but the determination to succeed will not falter.

Text-Dependent Questions

1. What government building did American Airlines Flight 77 hit?
2. At the time of the September 11 attacks, what country was housing Osama bin Laden?
3. What new terrorist group formed in 2013?

Research Projects

1. Research how ISIS uses social media to recruit new members and to target potential victims. What are countermeasures to each method?
2. Research the National September 11 Memorial and Museum. Where is it located and how has it commemorated the September 11 attacks?

Series Glosssary

Air marshal: Armed guard traveling on an aircraft to protect the passengers and crew; the air marshal is often disguised as a passenger.

Annexation: To incorporate a country or other territory within the domain of a state.

Armory: A supply of arms for defense or attack.

Assassinate: To murder by sudden or secret attack, usually for impersonal reasons.

Ballistic: Of or relating to firearms.

Biological warfare: Also known as germ warfare, this is war fought with biotoxins—harmful bacteria or viruses that are artificially propagated and deliberately dispersed to spread sickness among an enemy.

Cartel: A combination of groups with a common action or goal.

Chemical warfare: The use of poisonous or corrosive substances to kill or incapacitate the enemy; it differs from biological warfare in that the chemicals concerned are not organic, living germs.

Cold War: A long and bitter enmity between the United States and the Free World and the Soviet Union and its Communist satellites, which went on from 1945 to the collapse of Communism in 1989.

Communism: A system of government in which a single authoritarian party controls state-owned means of production.

Conscription: Compulsory enrollment of persons especially for military service.

Consignment: A shipment of goods or weapons.

Contingency operations: Operations of a short duration and most often performed at short notice, such as dropping supplies into a combat zone.

Counterintelligence: Activities designed to collect information about enemy espionage and then to thwart it.

Covert operations: Secret plans and activities carried out by spies and their agencies.

Cyberterrorism: A form of terrorism that seeks to cause disruption by interfering with computer networks.

Democracy: A government elected to rule by the majority of a country's people.

Depleted uranium: One of the hardest known substances, it has most of its radioactivity removed before being used to make bullets.

Dissident: A person who disagrees with an established religious or political system, organization, or belief.

Embargo: A legal prohibition on commerce.

Emigration: To leave one country to move to another country.

Extortion: The act of obtaining money or other property from a person by means of force or intimidation.

Extradite: To surrender an alleged criminal from one state or nation to another having jurisdiction to try the charge.

Federalize/federalization: The process by which National Guard units, under state command in normal circumstances, are called up by the president in times of crisis to serve the federal government of the United States as a whole.

Genocide: The deliberate and systematic destruction of a racial, political, or cultural group.

Guerrilla: A person who engages in irregular warfare, especially as a member of an independent unit carrying out harassment and sabotage.

Hijack: To take unlawful control of a ship, train, aircraft, or other form of transport.

Immigration: The movement of a person or people ("immigrants") into a country; as opposed to emigration, their movement out.

Indict: To charge with a crime by the finding or presentment of a jury (as a grand jury) in due form of law.

Infiltrate: To penetrate an organization, like a terrorist network.

Infrastructure: The crucial networks of a nation, such as transportation and communication, and also including government organizations, factories, and schools.

Insertion: Getting into a place where hostages are being held.

Insurgent: A person who revolts against civil authority or an established government.

Internment: To hold someone, especially an immigrant, while his or her application for residence is being processed.

Logistics: The aspect of military science dealing with the procurement, maintenance, and transportation of military matériel, facilities, and personnel.

Matériel: Equipment, apparatus, and supplies used by an organization or institution.

Militant: Having a combative or aggressive attitude.

Militia: a military force raised from civilians, which supports a regular army in times of war.

Narcoterrorism: Outrages arranged by drug trafficking gangs to destabilize government, thus weakening law enforcement and creating conditions for the conduct of their illegal business.

NATO: North Atlantic Treaty Organization; an organization of North American and European countries formed in 1949 to protect one another against possible Soviet aggression.

Naturalization: The process by which a foreigner is officially "naturalized," or accepted as a U.S. citizen.

Nonstate actor: A terrorist who does not have official government support.

Ordnance: Military supplies, including weapons, ammunition, combat vehicles, and maintenance tools and equipment.

Refugee: A person forced to take refuge in a country not his or her own, displaced by war or political instability at home.

Rogue state: A country, such as Iraq or North Korea, that ignores the conventions and laws set by the international community; rogue states often pose a threat, either through direct military action or by harboring terrorists.

Sortie: One mission or attack by a single plane.

Sting: A plan implemented by undercover police in order to trap criminals.

Surveillance: To closely watch over and monitor situations; the USAF employs many different kinds of surveillance equipment and techniques in its role as an intelligence gatherer.

Truce: A suspension of fighting by agreement of opposing forces.

UN: United Nations; an international organization, of which the United States is a member, that was established in 1945 to promote international peace and security.

Chronology

1775: June 14, the Continental Army is formed, the first army of the United States.

1775–1783: The Continental Army fights in the Revolutionary War, helping to free the United States from British rule; it is officially disbanded on November 2, 1783, and thereafter becomes the U.S. Army.

1787: The U.S. Constitution is written; President George Washington becomes the Army's commander in chief.

1812–1815: The U.S. Army fights against the British in the War of 1812.

1812: West Point Military academy is established.

1846–1848: The U.S. Army fights and wins the Mexican-American War.

1861–1865: The U.S. Civil War; the Union Army eventually defeats the Confederate Army.

1916: The National Defense Act authorizes the army to expand to 175,000 men in 111 regiments.

1917–1918: The U.S. Army enters World War I as part of the American Expeditionary Force led by General John J. Pershing; soldier numbers reach nearly four million men.

1940: Conscription is introduced, bringing the U.S. Army to a strength of 1.6 million men.

1941: December 7, the Japanese attack Pearl Harbor, and the United States enters World War II.

1945: September, World War II officially ends; over 11 million U.S. Army soldiers have served during the war.

1947: The U.S. Army Air Force splits away from the army to become the U.S. Air Force.

1950–1953: The U.S. Army goes to war again, this time in Korea as part of an international UN army against the Communists.

1961–1973: The U.S. Army becomes steadily involved in the Vietnam War.

1973–1990: The U.S. Army conducts combat missions and peacekeeping operations in areas around the world, including Grenada, the Middle East, and Panama.

1990–1991: In the biggest mission since Vietnam, the U.S. Army forms a massive part of an Allied force that liberates Kuwait during the Gulf War.

1995–1999: U.S. troops conduct peacekeeping and humanitarian operations in the territories of the former Yugoslavia, Europe.

2001–2014: U.S. special forces fight the Al Qaeda terrorist network in Afghanistan and prepare for more international operations in the war against terrorism. Operation New Dawn begins in 2010 as U.S. troops begin to be withdrawn.

2013– : U.S. special forces assist in the fight against the ISIS terrorist network in Iraq.

Further Resources

Websites

U.S. Department of Defense: www.defenselink.mil

U.S. Army main website www.army.mil

U.S. Army recruitment site: www.goarmy.com

National Guard: www.arng.army.mil

Reserve Officer Training Corps: www.armyrotc.com

U.S. Army weapons: usmilitary.about.com/cs/armyweapons/

Further Reading

Beckwith, Charlie A. and Donald Knox. *Delta Force: The Army's Elite Counter-Terrorist Unit.* New York, NY: Avon, 2000.

Bowden, Mark. *Black Hawk Down: A Story of Modern War.* New York, NY: Signet, 2000.

Harclerode, Peter and Mike Dewar. *Secret Soldiers: Special Forces in the War Against Terrorism.* New York NY: Cassell Academic, 2001.

Kurtz, Henry. U.S. *Army.* Brookfield, CT: Econo-Clad Books, 1999.

Nelson, Harold (ed.). *The Army.* Southport, CT: Hugh Lauter Levin Associates, 2001.

Netanyahu, Benjamin. *Fighting Terrorism: How Democracies Can Defeat Domestic and International Terrorists.* New York, NY: Noonday Press, 1997.

U.S. *Department of the Army Handbook.* New York, NY: International Business Publications, 2001.

Recruitment Information

To become a full-time regular soldier in the U.S. Army, you need to be between the ages of 17 and 35, a U.S. citizen or registered alien, and in good physical shape. For the Army Reserve, the criteria are the same, except that the upper age limit is reduced to 34. Army officers are recruited through a university or college participating in the Reserve Officer Training Corps, the Officer Candidate School, or the United States Military Academy at West Point. To inquire about any of these opportunities, go to a local army recruiting office or visit the website www.goarmy.com.

Index

Africa 21, 27, 57–58, 60
Air Force, U.S. 59, 76
Al Qaeda 66–68, 77
anthrax 51, 54

bin Laden, Osama 66
biological warfare 51–52, 54–55, 72
Bush, President George W. 66

chain of command 19–20
China 25, 51
Cold War 15, 72
Commands, Major 21–23, 26, 52
conscription 14, 72, 76
counterterrorism see terrorism 16, 21, 25, 57, 63–66, 68, 71, 73–74, 77

Department of Defense 19–20
drill sergeants (DSs) 31–34

engineers, military 23, 57, 70

federal army 10
    Afghanistan 16, 21, 23, 57, 66–69, 71, 77
    Civil War 10, 76
    Grenada 59–60, 63, 76
    Gulf War 16, 25, 41, 44–45, 47, 53, 57–58, 70, 77
    Korean War 15–16, 57
    Mexican War 10
    Mogadishu, Somalia 60–61, 70
    Vietnam War 15, 44, 57–58, 76
    War of 1812 10, 76
    World War I 12–14, 76
    World War II 14–16, 56–58, 60, 76

humanitarian work see operations other
        than war (OOTWs) 16, 21, 25–26, 57–58,
        60, 63, 77

Iraq 41, 51, 54, 66, 74, 77

Joint Chiefs of Staff 20, 28, 67

National Guard see reserve army 11, 14, 22, 25, 73
North Atlantic Treaty Organization (NATO) 21, 74
nuclear weapons 51–52

operations other than war (OOTWs) see humanitarian
        work 16, 21, 25–26, 57–58, 60, 63, 77

Pentagon Building, Washington, D.C. 65
physical fitness 35–38, 78

Rangers 58–63, 67–71
recruits 31–37, 70, 78
reserve army see National Guard 11, 14, 22, 25, 73
Reserve Officer Training Corps (ROTC) 38

September 11, 2001 51, 54, 65
soldiers, qualities 57–58, 63
South America 26
Soviet Union 15, 72
space-based technologies 26, 52
Special Operations Forces 67–70
state militias 9–10

Taliban 66–68
terrorism see counterterrorism 16, 21, 25, 57, 63–66, 68,
        71, 73–74, 77
Theater High-Altitude Area Defense (THAAD) 52–53
training 20–21, 23–24, 26, 31–32, 34–35, 38, 50
    basic training 29, 38
    chemical warfare 55
    combat 30–31, 33–34–35, 37
    fitness 33, 35
    special forces 70

Washington, D.C. 23, 65
Washington, George 9, 76
weapons and equipment
    airplanes 44
    ballistic missiles 51–52
    Black Hawk helicopter 62
    M16A2 rifle 34–35, 48
    M230 chain gun 44
    MH-47 Chinook helicopter 68
    MLRS M270 multiple launch rocket system 45
    Objective Individual Combat Weapon (OICW) 48
    Sidewinder air-to-air missiles 44
    space-based 26, 52
weapons of mass destruction (WMD) 51, 54
West Point military academy 10, 38, 76
World Trade Center, New York 64–65

About the Author

Dr. Chris McNab has written and edited numerous books on military history and the world's elite military forces. His list of publications to date includes *The Illustrated History of the Vietnam War, German Paratroopers of World War II, The World's Best Soldiers, The Elite Forces Manual of Endurance Techniques,* and *How to Pass the SAS Selection Course.* Chris's research into these titles has brought him into contact with many of the world's elite units, including the U.S. Marines and British Special Forces. Chris has also contributed to the field of military technology with publications such as *Weapons of War: AK47, Twentieth Century Small Arms, and Modern Military Uniforms.* His editorial projects include *The Battle of Britain* and *Fighting Techniques of the U.S. Marines 1941–45.* Chris lives in South Wales, U.K.

About the Consultant

Manny Gomez, an expert on terrorism and security, is President of MG Security Services and a former Principal Relief Supervisor and Special Agent with the FBI. He investigated terrorism and espionage cases as an agent in the National Security Division. He was a certified undercover agent and successfully completed Agent Survival School. Chairman of the Board of the National Law Enforcement Association (NLEA), Manny is also a former Sergeant in the New York Police Department (NYPD) where he supervised patrol and investigative activities of numerous police officers, detectives and civilian personnel. Mr. Gomez worked as a uniformed and plainclothes officer in combating narcotics trafficking, violent crimes, and quality of life concerns. He has executed over 100 arrests and received Departmental recognition on eight separate occasions. Mr. Gomez has a Bachelor's Degree and Master's Degree and is a graduate of Fordham University School of Law where he was on the Dean's list. He is admitted to the New York and New Jersey Bar. He served honorably in the United States Marine Corps infantry.